Creating with

VINYL CUTTERS

CATHLEEN SMALL

Published in 2017 by The Rosen Publishing Group, Inc.
29 East 21st Street, New York, NY 10010

Library of Congress Cataloging-in-Publication Data

Names: Small, Cathleen, author.
Title: Creating with vinyl cutters / Cathleen Small.
Description: First edition. | New York : Rosen Publishing, 2017. | Series: Getting creative with Fab Lab | Audience: Grades 5 to 8. | Includes bibliographical references and index.
Identifiers: LCCN 2016017428 | ISBN 9781508173502 (library bound)
Subjects: LCSH: Cutting machines—Technological innovations—Juvenile literature. | Vinyl polymers—Juvenile literature. | Makerspaces—Juvenile literature. | Technological innovations—Juvenile literature.
Classification: LCC TJ1230 .S655 2017 | DDC 621.9—dc23
LC record available at https://lccn.loc.gov/2016017428

Manufactured in China

Contents

Introduction

Years ago, creative kids would hunt around the house and garage for materials to build whatever creation was taking shape in their mind: tree houses, cars, robots, you name it. Sometimes they'd work together with friends or other kids from the neighborhood, and sometimes they'd work alone. They used the tools and materials at their disposal to bring their creations to life.

Today that innovation has taken the next step in the form of Fab Labs. These hands-on labs, which are popping up around the world, take the creativity of building stuff and combine it with access to cutting-edge technology. Kids who built robots out of cardboard and scrap metal in their parents' workshops a couple of decades ago can now go to a Fab Lab and use machines such as 3D printers, laser systems, milling machines, and vinyl cutters to make their robots even more elaborate and intricate.

The vinyl cutter is just one piece of equipment in a Fab Lab. But it's a versatile piece. You can create craft projects using only a vinyl cutter, such as T-shirts, decals, and elaborate cut-paper designs, or you can use the vinyl cutter in conjunction with other machines in the Fab Lab to create an even more detailed and developed project.

In this Fab Lab at Boston's South End Technology Center, students work with a STEM educator on using the laser cutter.

Years ago, vinyl cutters were machines used only in professional shops, where stickers were manufactured or clothing was created. Now, students using Fab Labs have access to vinyl cutters to enhance their projects.

FAB LABS: AN OVERVIEW

In the mid-twentieth century, home economics and shop classes were standard offerings in schools. Girls usually took home ec—cooking and sewing—while guys took shop—wood-shop and metal shop. As the century progressed, the gender lines began to fade, and schools began to see girls taking shop classes along with guys. It was still a male-dominated area of education for sure, but doors were beginning to open.

Today there is a strong push to give girls access to more STEM (science, technology, engineering, and mathematics) curricula, and guys are finding more access to arts curricula. (In fact, the STEM acronym is sometimes spelled STEAM, to incorporate arts into that science/technology/engineering/mathematics educational model.)

This is abundantly evident in Fab Labs, which are popping up across the country and around the globe. Currently, there are more than one hundred Fab Labs in production worldwide.

Fab Labs: What Are They?

Fab Labs are the brainchild of MIT's Center for Bits and Atoms. They are labs where people can use industrial-grade equipment, tools, and software to innovate, create, learn, and play. Basically, if you can think it, you can build it in a Fab Lab—from silkscreened T-shirts to architectural scale models to robotic arms. The question is, of course, how you build it. But that's up to you. Fab Labs provide standard equipment and software tools to allow users to create amazing projects of their own design.

Items you can create in a Fab Lab include miniatures, like this chair, and other intricately cut materials.

Fab Labs are available to people of most ages. The exact age of participants will depend on the specific Fab Lab, but in general they are open to children from about age eight and up. (In some labs, children under a certain age must be accompanied by an adult.) The beauty of a Fab Lab is in collaboration. Fab Labs across the globe are stocked with the same tools and equipment, which means that someone working in a Fab Lab in, say, California can collaborate and learn from (or teach!) someone working in a Fab Lab in, say, Japan. Invention doesn't take place in a bubble—it is nearly always inspired by our work with others. The global nature of Fab Labs ensures that users can work with other like-minded people to realize their inventions and creations.

Fab Labs Versus Other Creation Spaces

There are other organizations and groups that provide a similar sort of collaborative approach to learning and design. At the school level, for example, Odyssey of the Mind encourages groups of students to work together to design, create, and build using any materials at hand. And at a more global level, there are hackerspaces, makerspaces, TechShops, and Fab Labs. How can you tell the difference?

Hackerspaces gained popularity in Germany and Europe before spreading to the United States. They were originally groups of programmers sharing a physical space while they worked, thus allowing them to share ideas. Eventually, they began to add circuit design and manufacturing, as well as prototyping, to their programming. But hackerspaces are, at their core, more focused on programming.

ODYSSEY OF THE MIND: STUDENT-LED CREATION

If you don't have access to a Fab Lab but you're interested in the sort of collaborative design experience that a Fab Lab offers, Odyssey of the Mind (OotM) is a good place to start. It's an international program that encourages students in kindergarten through college to work together to design and build creative solutions to problems. The problems presented each year lend themselves to the same type of STEAM education that Fab Labs support, although students aren't presented with a gleaming lab full of high-end tools and software. In OotM, students create and innovate using whatever materials they have on hand or can acquire within a very limited budget. So an OotM student might build a "robot" out of cardboard repurposed from a team member's garage, whereas a Fab Lab student might build an actual working robot using the tools and software provided in the Fab Lab.

Still, the spirit and concepts are similar: people work together to creatively design and implement solutions to problems. And just as Fab Labs allow users a fair amount of autonomy in their work, Odyssey of the Mind encourages— make that requires—students to do all of the design and implementation. Parent coaches are only there to make sure no one gets injured in the process!

Makerspaces are more similar to Fab Labs in that they focus more on physical creation than hackerspaces tend to. But makerspaces don't necessarily adhere to the strict list of tools and software as inventory that a recognized Fab Lab does. Anyone can set up a makerspace with the tools that are appropriate to what they want to offer, whereas in a Fab Lab there is a set inventory of tools that must be available to users.

Fab Labs were born at MIT's Center for Bits and Atoms and now exist worldwide.

Even more similar to Fab Labs are TechShops. These began near Stanford in California, at one of the nation's seats of the tech industry. Much like Fab Labs, TechShops offer high-end equipment to their users. However, unlike Fab Labs, TechShops charge membership fees.

Fab Labs began just before TechShops did and at MIT's Center for Bits and Atoms. While TechShops are for-profit enterprises, Fab Labs are generally run by nonprofits and tend to be geared more toward teaching children than TechShops are. And Fab Labs have a stricter list of tools that must be offered than TechShops do. To qualify as a Fab Lab, an establishment needs to offer a very specific set of tools and software.

What You'll Find in a Fab Lab

A true Fab Lab isn't just a collection of random tools and items. Other creation and prototyping labs exist that have a similar spirit to Fab Labs, but for a lab to be *officially* considered a Fab Lab, it must meet four requirements:

- It must be free (or available by bartering) to the public at least part of each week.
- It must support the Fab Lab charter (available at the fabfoundation.org website).
- It must use a set of tools and processes common to other Fab Labs.
- It must be a part of the global Fab Lab network of knowledge sharing.

So what are these common tools that Fab Labs possess? While Fab Labs are indeed focused on digital fabrication, a Fab Lab goes far beyond simply housing a 3D printer and offering it to the public for use.

3D Printers

A Fab Lab is certainly more than just a 3D printer, but a 3D printer is indeed part of the lab. A 3D printer allows the user to "print" a three-dimensional object by applying powder in layers that build into the designated shape. Just as ink settles on paper to create two-dimensional printing, this powder settles in many, many layers to create the third dimension necessary to create an object.

FabFoundation.org recommends two possible 3D printers. The first is the Sindoh DP200 3DWOX, and the second is the Ultimaker2. Any Fab Lab you visit should have one of these two 3D printers and the associated cartridges, filaments, and other parts to go with it.

Both printers help you accomplish similar goals, although their technical specifications differ slightly, and their prices do as well, with the Ultimaker2 being more than twice the cost of the 3DWOX. Both are supported by Windows and Mac OS operating systems, and the Ultimaker2 is also supported by the Linux platform.

Laser Systems

Laser systems allow users to engrave on different types of materials, such as wood, glass, and stone. They can also be used to cut through plastic and other materials up to a certain thickness.

All Fab Labs will also have a laser system, though there are a few options. FabFoundation.org recommends from Epilog Lasers the:

- Mini 24
- Helix
- CO2
- Fusion M2

President Barack Obama admires the work done with a laser system at a TechShop in Pittsburgh, Pennsylvania.

Alternatively, FabFoundation.org recommends from Trotec Lasers the:

- Speedy 100
- Speedy 400

Or from GCC Lasers, FabFoundation.org recommends the:

- LaserPro Spirit LS
- LaserPro C180II

Regardless of which laser system your Fab Lab has, the lab will also have all of the associated pumps and attachments.

Milling Machine

FabFoundation.org recommends that each Fab Lab have two types of mills: a large CNC (computer numerical controlled) mill for creating furniture and housing, and an NC (numerical controlled) mini-mill for making circuits and casting molds. The mini-mill is generally tabletop size and can drill holes and mill small parts. The larger CNC mill is a freestanding piece of equipment that can carve designs and lettering, as well as make complicated cuts in wood when creating furniture.

For the large CNC mill, FabFoundation.org recommends either the open-loop ShopBot or the closed-loop ShopBot. Closed-loop ShopBots cost several thousand dollars more but are preferred; however, either variety of large CNC mill is acceptable in a Fab Lab, and the lab will also have all of the accessories and the dust collector needed for the mill.

FabFoundation.org gives three possibilities for mini-mills. All are from Roland: the SRM-20, the MDX-40A, and the MDX-540. The MDX-540 costs nearly three times as much as the MDX-40A and nearly four times as much as the SRM-20, but is supposed

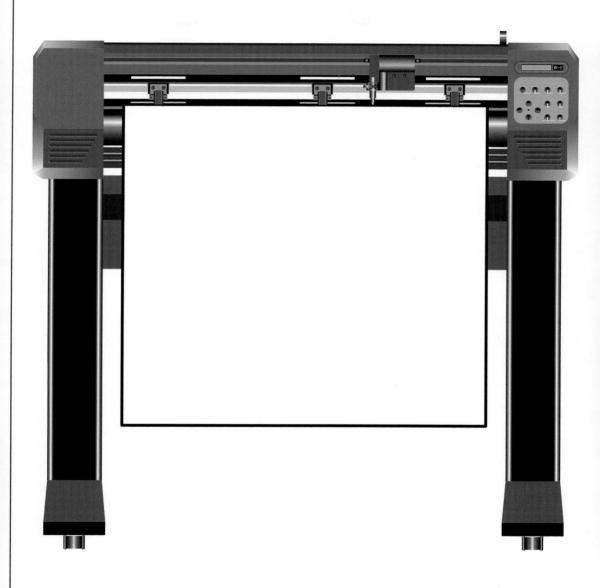

A vinyl cutter is a large machine that looks quite a bit like a plotter. In fact, it works like a plotter, but with a knife instead of ink.

to be superb in quality and performance. The SRM-20 is the entry-level mini-mill for a Fab Lab.

Vinyl Cutter

All Fab Labs should also have a vinyl cutter. These devices cut vinyl, as their name suggests, but they can usually also cut other thin materials, such as cloth, cardboard, and thin metals.

FabFoundation.org recommends either the Roland CAMM-1 GS-24 or the GCC Jaguar IV. They are similarly priced, and while their technical specifications differ slightly, both are excellent cutters that allow users to design and create a wide variety of projects.

Although the 3D printer in a Fab Lab might seem a bit more exciting than a vinyl cutter, the neat thing about the vinyl cutter is that it can be used in conjunction with the other tools in the lab. For example, you might use the 3D printer to build a scale model, but you'll use the vinyl cutter to create the decals that enhance your plain model. You can use the vinyl cutter on its own to create a variety of projects, but it can also be an infinitely useful tool when paired with other machines in the Fab Lab.

Other Tools Found in a Fab Lab

All Fab Labs also include electronics workbenches and numerous electronic components and programming tools to allow users to make full use of the machines available. The specific components and tools available in each Fab Lab may vary, but in general any recognized Fab Lab should have a wide array of tools to offer its users.

Computers and Software

Because Fab Labs are designed around digital fabrication, a software-driven process, all Fab Labs must have computers on which to run the software associated with any given tool. Although many of the tools in a Fab Lab use Mac-compatible software, Fab Labs generally use PCs because the Windows and Linux platforms are more universally compatible than the Mac OS platform. FabFoundation.org includes Windows-based applications in their recommended software because some institutions require it, but the foundation states that it "believe[s] in the open source approach" of Linux applications. Open-source software is typically easily accessible on the Web. Chances are your Fab Lab may already have the application you need, but if not you can put your research skills to use and find it on the internet.

The software used in a Fab Lab includes 2D design programs, vector-drawing programs, 3D design packages, and audio/video software. Examples include Photoshop, Illustrator, FreeCAD, AutoCAD, CorelDRAW, Maya, and Audacity.

Locating a Fab Lab

So now that you know all about Fab Labs and you're eager to get started working in one, the question is where do you find a recognized Fab Lab? Luckily, their locations are widespread—everywhere from Afghanistan to Thailand to the United States. The FabFoundation.org website features a page dedicated to finding a Fab Lab near you. There are Fab Labs in more than half of the fifty United States, as well as the District of Columbia.

If you can't find a Fab Lab near you, talk to an educational facility about possibly starting one. Although a fully equipped Fab Lab costs into the six figures according to FabFoundation.org, the United States Fab Lab Network suggests that organizations can consider starting a mini Fab Lab for much less.

If that's not an option, you can always check out a hackerspace, makerspace, TechShop, or Odyssey of the Mind group to give you a taste of what a Fab Lab can offer. The experience won't be exactly the same, of course, but it will at least allow you to dip your toe in the water until you can find a Fab Lab near you.

VINYL CUTTING IN A FAB LAB

If you've never worked in a Fab Lab or similar creation studio before, the idea of a vinyl cutter might be a bit cloudy to you. The name makes it rather obvious what it does—it cuts vinyl!—but what does that mean to you as a creator?

Think of a vinyl cutter as a plotter that uses a blade instead of a pen. A plotter is a device that allows you to create a complex digital drawing, which the machine then "plots" on a large piece of paper using a pen. You draw it electronically, and the machine prints it for you. A vinyl cutter works similarly—you create a complex (or simple, if you prefer!) design, but instead of drawing your design on paper, the vinyl cutter uses a sharp blade to cut it out of vinyl, vellum, cardboard, cardstock, fabric, or thin metal. With some vinyl cutters, such as the Roland CAMM-1 GS-24 model often used in Fab Labs, you can even cut magnetic materials to create your own custom-designed magnets.

CAD specialists and drafters use plotters to draw plans and blueprints.

Basically, if you can think it and create it on the computer, the vinyl cutter can produce it for you!

Vinyl Cutter Creations

The possibilities are nearly endless for what you can do with a vinyl cutter in a Fab Lab. Because Fab Labs provide high-quality vinyl cutting machines and the materials that go along with them, you have a lot of freedom in what you can design and create, from signs to stickers to cut paper to apparel. Chapter 3 will provide some specific ideas of projects you might create using the vinyl cutter in a Fab Lab, but in this chapter you can explore the general possibilities.

Signs and Banners

You can use a vinyl cutter to create custom signs and banners. If your Fab Lab uses a Roland CAMM-1 GS-24 vinyl cutter, you can create signs and banners up to 22.9 inches (58 centimeters) wide and 984.25 inches (2,499 cm) long. If your Fab Lab uses a GCC Jaguar IV, you'll be able to create slightly wider signs and banners, depending on the model of Jaguar IV. Regardless of which type of vinyl cutter your Fab Lab uses, you'll be able to create large, eye-catching signs.

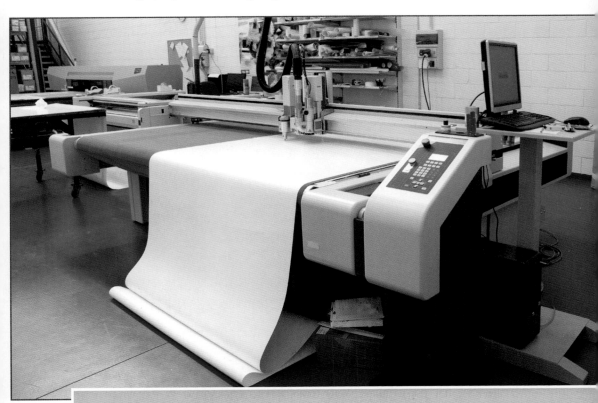

This flatbed cutter takes up quite a bit of space, but it can produce very large vinyl cuttings.

So what sort of sign might you create? If you're working on a school project, you might need a sign to announce a candidate for student council: "Vote John for Student Body President!" Or you might create a banner for a fund-raiser your school is holding. Or perhaps to advertise yearbook sales. The possibilities really are endless. Back in the day, you had to get a long piece of butcher paper and some markers or paints and set to work designing your banner. And those homespun signs had a certain charm and appeal, but they can't compare to the professional pop of a banner created on a vinyl cutter.

You can order vinyl banners from professional establishments, of course, but they are costly. Vistaprint, which tends to be a fairly low-priced website for printing, charges a starting price of more than $33 for a 2.5-foot (76 cm) by 6-foot (182 cm) banner. Using your Fab Lab's vinyl cutter, you could create that for free— and you'd have more design flexibility as well, since sites such as Vistaprint tend to rely on design templates or have some restrictions on your custom designs.

Stickers

Vinyl cutters are great for creating custom stickers, too. You can certainly create a simple sticker in a geometric shape, such as a circle or square, but the vinyl cutters in a Fab Lab will let you do far more than that. When you design your sticker, you can use creative fonts and intricate designs, and the vinyl cutter will cut even the smallest, tightest angles seamlessly. This opens up a world of possibilities to you.

One use for this tool might be creating decals for scale models. Have you ever looked at the tiny decals placed on model cars or airplanes, for example? You could use the vinyl cutter in a Fab Lab to create tiny custom decals like those.

Or perhaps you want a larger sticker, but with very detailed, precise edges? Think about a tattoo, for example—depending on the design, the edges can be incredibly intricate. An eagle with its wings spread has dozens of curved edges to create. It would be nearly impossible to create a sticker like that when hand-cutting vinyl, but a vinyl cutter in a Fab Lab could handle the task with no issue.

Just as you might create signs or banners for a school election or fund-raiser, you might also want to create stickers to advertise the same function or event. Switch gears a bit with the vinyl cutter, and you can easily do both.

Paper Crafts and Projects

The vinyl cutter in your Fab Lab will also allow you to work with nearly any type of paper. You can even use cardstock or thin cardboard. And beyond just cutting, you can also crease, score, or perforate your paper project. This can be useful when you want to create something like a tear-off postcard or a greeting card.

A regular greeting card is easy to create, of course—you can do it with a simple color printer and a piece of cardstock. But using a vinyl cutter lets you take it to the next level. Have you seen three-dimensional greeting cards, the ones you open and something pops out at you? Those are easy to create using a vinyl cutter. You can cut out small, intricate designs of objects to layer on the greeting card, or you can score the card so that certain items fold out when the card is opened.

The scoring feature can also be useful for crafts such as origami (the Japanese art of paper folding) and *kirigami* (the Japanese art of paper cutting). Remember the snowflakes you created as a young child, when you'd fold up a piece of paper

Here, a vinyl cutter was used to make small, elaborately cut pictures for cards. As with these, some assembly is often required after the initial cutting.

and make cuts with scissors and then unfold the paper to reveal your masterpiece? The vinyl cutter in your Fab Lab will allow you to do the same type of paper cutting but create much more intricate designs.

Going back to the idea of a school election or fund-raiser, the perforation feature of the vinyl cutter could be useful for creating ballots or postcards for people to include with their donation. Donations are often tax-deductible, so you might create a tear-off postcard that allows the donor to keep half as the receipt for his or her donation, and return the other half with check or credit card information.

Apparel and Accessories

Vinyl cutters are great for silkscreen printing. There are many websites that will custom-print T-shirts, hoodies, tote bags, and the like, but they tend to be quite expensive. T-shirts, for example, tend to run around $20 for a relatively basic design on CafePress, a well-known site for custom apparel. But using your Fab Lab's vinyl cutter, you can do your own printing on clothing or accessories. You can generally find plain T-shirts, tote bags, hoodies, and related items for a relatively low price at craft supply stores, and then you can use the vinyl cutter to produce your custom design to be applied to your item. You basically create a stencil on the vinyl cutter, which you then use to apply the ink to the shirt or other item.

In a school setting, this can be great for creating team apparel. Maybe you're part of a creation team such as Odyssey of the Mind, and you want all of the

When produced with a vinyl cutter, a design like these butterflies can actually be used as a stencil and then applied to other materials through screen printing.

team members to have matching team shirts. Using the vinyl cutter in the Fab Lab, this is a simple and inexpensive project. Custom apparel can be a great fund-raiser, too. The cost outlay for plain T-shirts is fairly low, and if you create a custom design using the vinyl cutter, you can create shirts on demand and sell them at a higher price, with the profit going to whatever charity or event you're raising money for.

COLLABORATION AND ETIQUETTE

Collaboration can yield some brilliant ideas and creations, but it requires that the participants observe proper etiquette. It's one thing to share ideas and put them together to come up with a design; it's another thing altogether to listen to someone's ideas and appropriate them as your own. You wouldn't want it to happen to you, and you certainly don't want to do it to anyone else.

Make sure your dialogue with your collaborators is open and honest. If you like an idea and want to run with it, then do it together. Ask the person whose idea it was if you can work together on the project. If the person *doesn't* want to work with you but is willing to share his or her ideas and let you use them, then always give credit where it's due—let everyone know that your creation was inspired by the person who initially shared the idea with you. It's simply good manners to give credit to the person who originally came up with the idea, even if that person eventually abandons the idea and moves on.

And be sure to listen to and consider all ideas when you're collaborating. They may not all be great ideas, but don't dismiss any without consideration. Every idea at least deserves to be heard, even if the team ultimately decides not to pursue it.

Skills You'll Need to Work with a Vinyl Cutter

As you can see, you can use the vinyl cutter in your Fab Lab for innumerable projects and creations. But obviously, it's not as simple as just walking up and using the device. It's a large, expensive piece of machinery, so you're going to need some skills before you jump in on your first project.

Roland, the manufacturer of the CAMM-1 GS-24 vinyl cutter found in many Fab Labs, offers a Roland Academy training program for people who purchase their vinyl cutters. They have in-person workshops and webinars, and chances are someone in your Fab Lab has been trained in how to use the vinyl cutter. But as a participant in the Fab Lab, you won't need to go through the same detailed training as your Fab Lab administrator. Instead, the people working in the Fab Lab should be able to show you the basics.

A wood chisel, as seen here, is a simple tool, but flying woodchips could cause serious damage to the eyes.

You'll need to know the basics of some software, too. If your Fab Lab is using a Roland CAMM-1 GS-24 vinyl cutter, you'll need to use the Roland CutStudio software. You'll also likely use Adobe Illustrator and/or CorelDRAW. If your lab is using a GCC Jaguar IV vinyl cutter, FabFoundation.org recommends using the CorelDRAW software. You may also use Sure Cuts A Lot, SignPal, and/or GreatCut, as well as Adobe Illustrator or AutoCAD.

And of course you'll need to take basic safety precautions that you would take when working with any type of machinery. Wear safety glasses to protect your eyes. And it's always a good idea to remove rings, bracelets, and other hand/wrist accessories when you're working with a piece of machinery such as this.

Get Creative

The ideas presented in this chapter are just a few of the many, many things you can do with a vinyl cutter. And remember, you have the other tools in the Fab Lab at your disposal, too. Think about combining tools to create projects. Perhaps you use the 3D printer to create a scale model and then the vinyl cutter to create intricate decals for it. Or maybe you use the mini-mill to create tiny parts to enhance a kirigami design that you're creating with the vinyl cutter. If you can dream it, you can do it.

You probably have a lot of good ideas rolling around in your head, but eventually you may hit a block. The beauty of Fab Labs is that collaboration is encouraged, and you can work with other people in your Fab Labs or in Fab Labs around the world to create a joint project. Because every Fab Lab offers the same basic tools, collaboration is easy. And although it can be tempting to work on your own, remember that some of the most brilliant creations were the work of more than one mind. The original Apple computer is a good example. Where would Steve Jobs have been without Steve Wozniak as his collaborator? Nowadays, employees at Apple and similarly innovative companies work in teams, because it's a simple fact that collaboration can yield the best results. So when you get stuck, turn to the other members of the Fab Lab community, and see where it takes you!

Chapter THREE

FABULOUS FAB LAB PROJECTS

By now, you know what's available in a Fab Lab, and hopefully you've found one near you. You also know what a vinyl cutter does and what general sorts of projects you can do with it. You even know what sorts of skills you'll need to work with the vinyl cutter in a Fab Lab. So what's next? Getting started with projects, of course! The possibilities in a Fab Lab are limited only by your own imagination. If you're working on your own, start with a simple, beginner-level project and work your way up to something more challenging. Or, if you're a jump-right-in kind of person, you can collaborate with other people in the Fab Lab to start on a more complicated project. Wherever you decide to start, just make sure to work carefully and safely.

Beginner Projects

If you're just starting out in a Fab Lab, you'll probably want to begin with a simple project. It might not seem terribly exciting when you've spent time dreaming about the elaborate projects you can create in the Fab Lab, but it's a good way to get comfortable with the Fab Lab and with the machines and tools you'll be using in it.

SAFETY FIRST!

The specific safety guidelines for any given Fab Lab are determined by that particular lab. For example, the University of New Mexico School of Architecture and Planning's Fab Lab requires students to attend safety use and orientation training, pass a use and safety training test, and sign a safety form to gain access to the lab. The safety certification is then good for three years of Fab Lab use. The Mott Community College Fab Lab in Michigan simply requires students to pass a safety module. And the Fab Lab at Mohawk Valley Community College doesn't have any specific safety tests for users to pass, but they caution students to follow general workshop safety precautions.

In general, standard workshop safety precautions are recommended in any Fab Lab. Users are advised not to wear jewelry, neckties, long sleeves, open-toed shoes, or loose-fitting clothing. Long hair should be pulled back or secured under a hat. Safety glasses and ear protection should be worn when using any equipment. Facemasks should be worn when users are working with a machine that will generate dust or particles, such as a sander. And each machine will have specific safety precautions that you should follow at all times.

Stickers and Temporary Tattoos

Creating vinyl stickers is a very simple Fab Lab project. You slide the vinyl sheet you've chosen into the vinyl cutter, vinyl side up, and ensure that it's aligned straight. The vinyl cutter will scan the vinyl sheet for size and thickness and provide those values so you can enter those in the associated software you're using. If you're using the Roland GX-24, this will be the Roland CutStudio software, and you can even click a button to have the software pull the dimensions from the cutter itself. You can then design the sticker using any of the tools in the robust software package;

Once you have created your design and programmed the software, you can sit back and watch the vinyl cutter work its magic.

when you're finished, you simply output it to the waiting vinyl cutter, which will create your sticker.

Now comes the cool part: The vinyl cutter actually uses the thickness of the vinyl (which it determined earlier) to apply the exact amount of pressure to allow it to cut through the vinyl, but not through the backing sheet. When the cutting is finished, you can then "weed" out the sticker, which means pulling off all of the excess vinyl that's not part of your sticker. What will be left is a backing sheet with your sticker on it, ready to be peeled off and applied wherever you'd like.

If your sticker is composed of many small pieces (such as individual letters), you can use a special application film to apply all the pieces at once, in the correct order and spacing, rather than applying many separate pieces.

If your Fab Lab uses a GCC Jaguar IV vinyl cutter, the software process is a bit more manual. You'll use something like Adobe Illustrator or CorelDRAW and "print" your design to the vinyl cutter, rather than using proprietary software like the GX-24 uses. But the overall process is the same: you design the sticker and "print" it to the vinyl cutter, then weed out the excess vinyl and apply your sticker.

The process for creating temporary tattoos is quite similar, given that temporary tattoos are essentially a type of sticker! The main difference is that you use tattoo decal paper instead of traditional vinyl.

Wall Decorations

If you know how to make stickers, making wall decals will be easy. After all, they are essentially just large stickers. You'll likely be working with much larger pieces of vinyl for wall decals, though, which means you'll need to take extra care when loading

Wall decals are easy to create with a vinyl cutter, and they can add a unique style to your room or other living space.

the vinyl into the cutter. You don't want the large vinyl sheet feeding through crookedly or getting jammed.

After the cutter produces the finished wall decal, you'll need to weed the excess vinyl, just as you do with smaller stickers. You may need to use tweezers or an X-Acto knife for the more delicate areas. For a wall decal, you'll likely need to put on a layer of application tape or transfer tape. This will allow you to apply the decal to the wall smoothly, without the vinyl folding or bubbling. Putting on a layer of application tape is relatively simple and involves smoothing a large sheet of what often looks like masking tape over your decal.

Intermediate Projects

Once you've tried a beginner-level project, you can move on to something a bit more difficult. May people like to use vinyl cutters to create custom-designed graphics to apply to T-shirts and other apparel. A less common but equally fun project is using a vinyl cutter to create origami or kirigami.

T-Shirts and Other Apparel

To create graphic designs for clothing and accessories such as tote bags, the process is similar to creating stickers. You create a design just as you would for a sticker or a wall decal and use the Fab Lab's vinyl cutter to plot and cut the design. However, there is one crucial change in the steps: when you create your design, you then have to reverse the image so that it's a mirror of what you want the final product to look like. The reason why is, you'll be using heat-press or T-shirt vinyl, which you'll apply to your garment face down, with the application backing on top and ready to be peeled off after the vinyl is heated and cured so it sticks to the fabric.

After you've reversed and cut your design using the vinyl cutter, you'll need to weed out the excess vinyl so you are left with just the design you want on the clothing.

The next step is to use a heat press to warm up the fabric on the shirt or other piece of clothing. It doesn't take long—you just want to warm up the fabric a bit. It's a good idea to place a stiff piece of cardboard inside the garment to ensure that the fabric stays smooth and flat when you're working on it.

Then place your cut vinyl design on the fabric, vinyl side down, being careful to align everything just as you want it. Place the garment back in the heat press, cover it with a thin protective layer, such as Teflon, and apply heat for the recommended time for that particular transfer material (usually about twenty seconds). Then remove the garment, allow it to cool, and then carefully peel the backing off of the vinyl design. You'll be left with a professional-looking garment!

Origami and Kirigami

You can create folded or cut paper art, called origami or kirigami, using your vinyl cutter. Adobe Illustrator has plug-ins you can download that will allow you to designate cuts, scores, and per-forations for your origami and kirigami creations.

If you have a project that incorporates cuts, scores, and perforations, you simply process the piece multiple times—once for cuts, once for scores, and once for perforations.

You might wonder why you'd use a vinyl cutter for a simple origami project, though. It makes sense for kirigami, which requires precision cutting, but why origami, which is just folding? One answer is that you can use a vinyl cutter to score the folding lines for a neater fold. Suppose you wanted to do a simple origami project with a class of kindergartners. Young children don't always have the fine-motor skills necessary to do careful folds, but if you scored their craft paper, they would likely be able to enjoy and complete the project.

A second answer is curved folds. Creating a curved fold by hand is quite difficult, but using a vinyl cutter you can achieve it. Artist Beth Johnson creates amazing origami designs with intricately curved folds. She uses a vinyl cutter to score the paper before she attempts the complex curved folds.

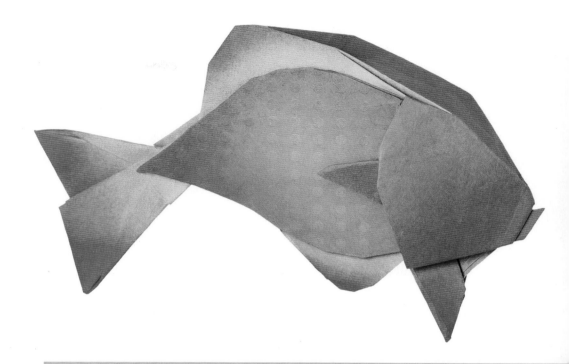

If the project you have in mind has any curved folds, like this origami fish, a vinyl cutter may be your new best friend.

Advanced Projects

If you're really feeling bold, why not try an advanced project with the vinyl cutter? Just be sure to ask the teacher or other professional working in the Fab Lab if you need help on the project.

Enhancements to 3D Scale Models

For an advanced project, why not incorporate multiple machines available in the Fab Lab? A model airplane is one such multi-tool project you could create. In store-bought varieties, model airplanes range from simple Revell kits filled with plastic parts that you glue together and decals that you affix, to highly detailed metal creations with working engines.

In the Fab Lab, you could go as simple or as high end as your imagination and skills take you. The 3D printer and laser systems will allow you to create model parts out of different materials, and you could use the mini-mill to make circuits if you decide to make your model with a working engine.

The vinyl cutter, then, would allow you to enhance your model with intricate decals. Even the simple Revell model airplane kits from the store come with tiny but elaborate decals to enhance the model; in the Fab Lab, you could create those decals yourself and get as creative as you want.

Naturally, you could do that with *any* 3D model you build in the Fab Lab—it doesn't have to be an airplane. If you're interested in architecture, you could create a 3D scale model of a building design using the 3D printer, laser system, and perhaps the CNC mill, depending on what material you're using. When it comes time to add all the sophisticated details to your architectural scale model, you can use the vinyl cutter to create them.

Copper Circuits

If you want to move beyond making vinyl decals and clothing embellishments, try making a copper circuit using a vinyl cutter. Vinyl cutters such as those found in a Fab Lab are designed to cut through copper tape, which you can use to create copper circuits.

You design your circuit in any sort of design software, such as Illustrator or CorelDRAW, and then you simply save it as a graphic image and output it to the vinyl cutter for cutting. You'll affix your final circuit to a heat-resistant surface and then, much like when you created a vinyl sticker, you'll weed out the unwanted pieces

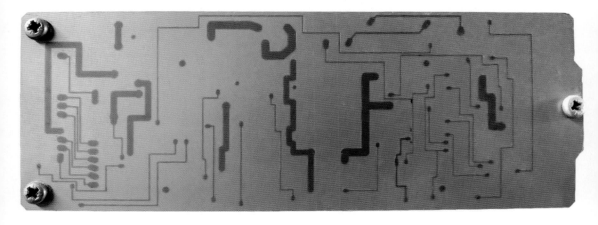

Circuits sound complicated, but it's surprisingly easy to create a simple circuit out of copper tape—especially if you have a vinyl cutter on hand to make the necessary cuts.

of copper tape. You will have to be careful soldering components onto your circuit because the surface to which you've affixed your circuit will get hot. Just take care to solder quickly, and you should be fine.

So what will you do with that circuit board you've created? That is completely up to you. The circuit board *will* conduct electricity, so you can use it to add electrical elements to the items you've designed in the Fab Lab. For example, if you decided to create a scale model of a car, you might use a copper circuit board to power a small set of headlights for your car.

The Beauty of Creativity

Perhaps the best part about working in a Fab Lab is that your creativity will spark more creative ideas in you. When you first set foot in the Fab Lab, you might have a couple of ideas rolling around in your head. But after you start working with the vinyl cutter and other machines and tools in the Fab Lab, your mind will start to churn with more possibilities. What you design today will influence what you design tomorrow and in the future, as you continue to work in the Fab Lab. Creativity breeds creativity, and no place is that more obvious than in the Fab Lab, where you have the tools at your disposal to bring your creativity to life!

Chapter FOUR

BEYOND THE FAB LAB

Fab Labs are a lot of fun. Where else will you find a space filled with high-quality tools you can use to create whatever you can dream up? And where else can you find a group of like-minded people to brainstorm and create with? Fab Labs are really a dreamer's paradise and an inventor's utopia.

But there's more to a Fab Lab than just having fun. The skills you acquire in a Fab Lab can take you far beyond the lab as you move forward in your future. They can ultimately result in a career for you, or even just a creative hobby.

Applying What You've Learned

This book has mostly discussed vinyl cutting in a Fab Lab, but your time in the lab will also allow you to experiment with milling machines, laser systems, and 3D printers, among other tools.

Did you find particular enjoyment in working with one or more of these tools? Is it something you might like to pursue in the future? If so, there are definitely career possibilities.

Career Opportunities

If a higher-education degree is your ultimate goal, Harvard University offers a digital fabrication and robotics graduate degree in their school of design. Students in the program work with different materials and design architectures and use robots

Harvard University's Graduate School of Design is one place where you can learn higher-level digital fabrication and robotics.

in the fabrication process. It's a computer-intensive program where students engage in extensive experimentation as they work on several research projects.

If your sights aren't set on a graduate degree from an Ivy League university, there are certainly plenty of other job possibilities in the digital fabrication industry. A recent job posting from the Fashion Institute of Technology, for example, sought a fabrication lab technician with an associate's or bachelor's degree and relevant industry experience. The City University of New York system had a related position open that required similar education and experience. And a well-known branding and marketing company offered entry-level positions as a digital fabrication assistant.

Whatever your educational goals are, there are careers to be found in digital fabrication. You can specialize in one area, such as vinyl cutting, or you can work in an environment that uses multiple fabrication tools and potentially gain a wider range of experience.

Job Outlook

The skills you acquire in a Fab Lab can translate to numerous careers. High-end careers such as architecture require fabrication skills that you can learn in a Fab Lab. But on the less school-intensive end of things, there are also entry-level careers such as metal and plastic machine workers, in which you work hands-on with machines similar to the ones you've used in the Fab Lab. These jobs generally require you to have a high school diploma, although in some cases a GED is acceptable. It's also preferred that you have a good background in math and computer courses. You'll generally get on-the-job training for the machines you're working with in this type of job, and in some cases there are certifications you can get to advance your earning potential.

In addition to math and computer skills, these entry-level machine-operator careers are physically taxing and require you to be in good physical shape to stand on your feet all day and work with heavy, bulky machinery. They also require dexterity, as you are sometimes working with designs that will require you to use precise hand movements to set the machines.

Naturally, the earning potential will be much higher if you choose to pursue an advanced degree such as the Harvard one and ultimately take a job in that field. For the more entry-level machine-operator jobs, the *Bureau of Labor Statistics Occupational Outlook Handbook 2016–2017* edition lists annual salaries anywhere from about $29,000 for entry-level machine setters to about $47,000 for programmers of CNC machines. The median annual wage for all metal and plastic machine workers as of May 2014 was listed at just over $33,000, which is just slightly below the median annual wage for all occupations in the United States.

The job outlook for the entry-level metal and plastic machine jobs isn't overly positive. Because more of these jobs are being done by computer and robot, the need for skilled laborers for them is declining. The Bureau of Labor Statistics projects a 13 percent decline in these jobs over the next decade. However, workers who are trained to operate computer numerically controlled machines, such as the CNC mills used in the Fab Lab, are expected to have a reasonably positive job outlook. It stands to reason—computers may replace the laborers, but someone needs to be able to operate the computers!

GOOD WORKS STUDIO

Two young architects from Houston have taken seriously their personal goal to do good for others. While in Rice University's Graduate School of Architecture, Scott Key and Sam Brisendine created Good Works Studio, Inc. They have since graduated and both work for Houston-area architecture firms, but they also run Good Works Studio, which pioneered the design of

(continued on the next page)

Scott Key (*left*) and Sam Brisendine's (*right*) Emergency Floor product is being installed in refugee camps worldwide.

(continued from the previous page)

Emergency Floor—a sustainable flooring system that uses the materials found in refugee camps to create flooring for displaced refugees.

Refugees in regions such as Nepal and the Middle East often have to sleep on the ground in camps, which puts them at risk of life-threatening conditions of infection, hypothermia, and flooding. By using the discarded shipping pallets found at refugee camps and placing over them a fabricated interlocking flooring, Good Works Studio has created a much safer environment for those people forced to live in refugee camps.

For these budding architects with their background in advanced fabrication, it was a simple solution to a very big problem. But to the thousands of refugees who no longer have to sleep on cold, disease-infected ground, it is life changing. You never know how the skills you acquire in a Fab Lab could someday end up helping a vulnerable population.

Doing Good

Thomas Jefferson once said that "every human mind feels pleasure in doing good to another." If doing good is important to you, you can put the knowledge you learned in a Fab Lab to good use.

Making signs and banners and stickers may not seem particularly philanthropic, but think for a moment about the entities who need those items. Sure, you'll have your everyday businesses and corporations, but you'll also have nonprofit organizations. There are nonprofit organizations for virtually *every* cause you can think of, and they all have need for promotional materials and things of that nature.

For example, Down Syndrome Connection of the Bay Area is a nonprofit organization that provides services and support for more than five hundred people with Down syndrome in the San Francisco Bay Area. Because they are a nonprofit organization with no government funding, they rely on grants and donations to keep their doors open. To get those grants and donations, they need to have their name out there and appear at fund-raisers and other events where potential donors may be found. As a part of that and the programs they run, the organization has numerous signs, banners, decals, magnets, detachable postcards, and other items created with—you guessed it!—a vinyl cutter.

So if you are interested in doing good and giving back to the community, think of some sort of organization or entity that is near and dear to your heart, and consider the creative ways you might be able to put your Fab Lab skills to work helping them.

Thinking Globally

On a global level, the skills you learn in a Fab Lab may contribute to what Dartmouth College professor of business Richard D'Aveni called "the next industrial revolution." In an interview with Yahoo! News, D'Aveni speculated that thanks to digital fabrication, mass-manufacturing industries would disappear in the next twenty-five years.

That means countries that offer many mass-manufacturing jobs might become irrelevant to our production economy— which is good and bad. Certainly, it would mean job loss in those countries. If a machine in the United States can do what a person in another country is currently doing, it's likely that the job will be

You don't have to be part of a mass manufacturer to use fabrication tools. If you live in a community with a Fab Lab, TechShop, makerspace, or other similar environment, then you can work in a fabrication environment.

done domestically, by machine, rather than outsourcing it to a human in another country. But it would also mean an end to child labor in some countries where children aren't protected by labor laws. It could mean decreased pollution, because the fabrication machines used in the United States would put out less pollutants than some of the factories currently used in other countries. And it would mean less in import costs for the United States, which currently pays to import many products from other countries.

As with many things, there's good and there's bad. The digital fabrication process is certainly revolutionary and has the potential to provide much benefit. However, that benefit won't be without some costs, too.

Looking Ahead

If you have the chance to participate in a Fab Lab, by all means do it! And explore all of the tools at your disposal. You might think one particular piece of equipment sounds the most interesting—maybe you're drawn to the 3D printer and want to spend your time using that. But don't discount the other pieces of equipment available to you in the Fab Lab. You never know what you'll ultimately find most enjoyable, and you can create some amazing projects if you use multiple tools.

Let your creativity run wild, and above all, have fun!

Glossary

autonomy Independence.

barter To exchange goods or services in trade, without the use of money.

brainchild A specific person's invention or idea.

curricula A course of study.

dexterity Skill in performing intricate fine-motor tasks, generally using the hands.

digital fabrication The creation of a product using a computer-controlled machine.

domestically In a home country.

etiquette Manners or polite behavior in a particular society.

heat press A machine that uses heat to apply a graphic or design to fabric.

Ivy League A group of prestigious universities located in the eastern United States.

median The midpoint of a given range.

nonprofit An organization that does not exist to make a profit. Any profits made are put back into the organization itself.

platform The computer system that allows programs on a computer to run. On Apple computers, the platform is Mac OS. Windows is a major platform for PCs. Linux is an open-source platform that can be used on both PCs and Macs.

prototyping Making a model of something. That model is then used to create more copies of the item.

refugee Someone who must leave their home to escape a negative situation, such as war or natural disaster.

scale model A smaller-sized model of a larger object. In scale models, all dimensions are typically reduced by the same ratio.

silkscreen A fine mesh screen that can be used to apply graphics to apparel.

solder To use melted metal to join metal objects.

template A pattern that can be used to create multiple copies of a given item.

utopia A place where everything is perfect. True utopia doesn't exist, but the term is applied to the idea of a perfect place.

vellum Fine calfskin parchment.

webinar An internet seminar.

X-Acto knife A small, very sharp knife used in crafts and projects that require fine, exact cuts.

Destination Imagination
1111 South Union Avenue
Cherry Hill, NJ 08002
(888) 321-1503
Website: http://www.destinationimagination.org
Much like Odyssey of the Mind, this organization poses academic problems to students in the areas of STEM, fine arts, and service. The students then work in teams to solve problems collaboratively and compete in a tournament.

Exploratorium
Pier 15
Embarcadero at Green Street
San Francisco, CA 94111
(415) 528-4444
Website: http://www.exploratorium.edu
The Exploratorium of San Francisco is a huge hands-on museum that focuses on learning through experience. The exhibits are focused on the areas of STEM, art, and human perception.

FabCentral
Center for Bits and Atoms
20 Ames Street, E15-404
Cambridge, MA 02139
(617) 253-4651
Website: http://cba.mit.edu
Much like Fab Foundation, this site supports the international network of Fab Labs. However, this site is maintained by MIT's Center for Bits and Atoms, where Fab Labs were created.

Fab Foundation
The Fab Foundation
50 Milk Street, 16th Floor
Boston, MA 02109
(857) 333-777
Website: http://www.fabfoundation.org
This nonprofit was founded in 2009 from the MIT Center for Bits
and Atoms and supports the Fab Lab network
internationally.

Maker Camp
Website: http://makercamp.com
Maker Camp is an online community that offers virtual camps
that allow students to create, tinker, and learn together. The
site also provides information about in-person camps in
communities around the globe.

Nspire
Website: http://nspire.org
This student-run nonprofit in Canada seeks to connect inspired
youth with entrepreneurs and industry professionals in the
business and technology sector.

Odyssey of the Mind
c/o Creative Competitions, Inc.
406 Ganttown Road
Sewell, NJ 08080
(856) 256-2797
Website: http://odysseyofthemind.com
This organization allows students from kindergarten through
college to participate in competitions that encourage them
to work as a team to create and innovate solutions to

problems. The teams are entirely student run, with parent coaches only to ensure safety.

Ontario Science Centre
770 Don Mills Road
Toronto, ON M3C 1T3
Canada
(416) 696-1000
Website: http://ontariosciencecentre.ca
This museum for everyone from children to teens to adults incorporates hands-on learning and experience. The Weston Family Innovation Centre at the museum is specifically dedicated to problem solving through experimentation.

Websites

Because of the changing nature of Internet links, Rosen Publishing has developed an online list of websites related to the subject of this book. This site is updated regularly. Please use this link to access the list:

http://www.rosenlinks.com/GCFL/vinyl

For Further Reading

Baker, Laura Berens. *Laser Cutting for Fashion and Textiles.* London, England: Laurence King Publishing, 2016.

Bernier, Samuel N., and Bertier Luyt. *Design for 3D Printing.* San Francisco, CA: Maker Media, Inc., 2015.

Burker, Josh. *The Invent to Learn Guide to Fun.* Constructing Modern Knowledge Press, 2015.

Ceceri, Kathy. *Paper Inventions.* San Francisco, CA: Maker Media, Inc., 2015.

Ceceri, Kathy. *Simple Robots.* San Francisco, CA: Maker Media, Inc., 2015.

Cohen, Jacob. Getting the Most Out of MakerSpaces to Build Robots. New York, NY: Rosen Publishing Group, 2014.

Frauenfelder, Mark, ed. Make: Technology on Your Time, Volume 40: New Maker Tools. Maker Media, Inc., 2014.

Gillespie, Maryann. *Craft Vinyl Decorating Ideas: Gifts, Home Décor, and Moneymaking Tips Galore.* CreateSpace Independent Publishing Platform, 2015.

Graves, Colleen, and Aaron Graves. *The Big Book of Makerspace Projects: Inspiring Makers to Experiment, Create, and Learn.* New York, NY: McGraw-Hill Education, 2016.

Hackett, Chris. *The Big Book of Maker Skills: Tools & Techniques for Building Great Tech Projects.* San Francisco, CA: Weldon Owen, 2014.

Holz, Angelika. *Crafty Cuttings: The Plotter's Compendium.* Angelika Holz, 2015.

Kloski, Liza Wallach, and Nick Kloski. *Getting Started with 3D Printing.* San Francisco, CA: Maker Media, Inc., 2016.

Weinstein, Noah. *Extraordinary Projects for Ordinary People: Do-It-Yourself Ideas from the People Who Actually Do Them.* New York, NY: Skyhorse Publishing, 2012.

Wilkinson, Karen, and Mike Petrich. *The Art of Tinkering.* San Francisco, CA: Weldon Owen, 2014.

Bibliography

Bureau of Labor Statistics. "Metal and Plastic Machine Workers." *U.S. Department of Labor, Occupational Outlook Handbook, 2016-17 Edition,* December 17, 2015 (http://www.bls.gov/ooh/production/metal-and-plastic-machine-workers.htm).

Cavalcanti, Gui. "Is It a Hackerspace, Makerspace, TechShop, or Fab Lab?" *Makezine,* May 22, 2013 (http://makezine.com/2013/05/22/the-difference-between-hackerspaces-makerspaces-techshops-and-fablabs/).

Cease, Maggie. "Beth Johnson Origami." *Maker Works*, May 21, 2014 (http://maker-works.com/beth-johnson-origami/).

Creative Competitions. "Odyssey of the Mind." Retrieved March 21, 2016 (http://www.odysseyofthemind.com/default.php).

Emergency Floor. "Emergency Floor." Retrieved March 22, 2016 (http://emergencyfloor.com).

Fab Foundation. "Fab Lab Inventory." Retrieved March 21, 2016 (https://docs.google.com/spreadsheets/d/1U-jcBWOJEjBT5A0N84IUubtcHKMEMtndQPLCkZCkVsU/pub?single=true&gid=0&output=html).

Fab Foundation. "The Hardware and Software." Retrieved March 21, 2016 (http://www.fabfoundation.org/fab-labs/setting-up-a-fab-lab/the-hardware-and-software/).

Fab Foundation. "Who/What Qualifies as a Fab Lab?" Retrieved March 21, 2016 (http://www.fabfoundation.org/fab-labs/fab-lab-criteria/).

GCC World. "Jaguar Vinyl Cutter." Retrieved March 21, 2106 (http://www.gccworld.com/goods.php?act=view&no=7).

Harvard University. "Digital Fabrication & Robotics." Retrieved March 22, 2016 (http://www.gsd.harvard.edu/#/academic-programs/master-in-design-studies/technology/digital-fabrication-robotics.html).

Instructables. "How to Make Circuits with a Roland CAMM Sign Cutter." Retrieved March 24, 2016 (http://www.instructables.com/id/How-to-make-circuits-with-a-Roland-CAMM-sign-cutte/?ALLSTEPS).

Jefferson, Thomas. Letter to John Adams, dated Oct 14, 1816. Reprinted on Founding.com. Retrieved March 22, 2016 (http://founding.com/founders-library/american-political-figures/thomas-jefferson/letter-to-john-adams/).

Mangels, John. "Equipping a Fab Lab." *Plain Dealer*, June 2009 (http://blog.cleveland.com/science_impact/2009/06/00cgFAB.pdf).

Mohawk Valley Community College. "FABLab Safety Protocol." Retrieved March 24, 2016 (http://www.mvcc.edu/stem-center/mvccfablab/fablab-safety-protocol).

Mott Community College FABLAB. "Safety, Use, and Procedures." Retrieved March 24, 2016 (http://mcc.edu/fablab/fab_safety.shtml).

Roland. "CAMM-1 GS-24 Desktop Cutter Specifications." Retrieved March 22, 2016 (https://www.rolanddga.com/products/vinyl-cutters/camm-1-gs-24-desktop-vinyl-cutter/specifications).

"SA+P Fab Lab Handbook 2013/2014." University of New Mexico School of Architecture and Planning, November 7, 2013 (https://saap.unm.edu/documents/fablab/2013-fablab-handbook.pdf).

Sigman, Michael. "Digital Fabrication: More Than the Stuff of Dreams." *Huffington Post,* August 6, 2013 (http://www.huffingtonpost.com/michael-sigman/digital-fabrication-more_b_3397489.html).

SignWarehouse.com. "A Basic Guide to T-Shirt Vinyl & Heat

Transfer Film." Retrieved March 24, 2016 (http://www.
signwarehouse.com/blog/basic-guide-to-t-shirt-vinyl
-and-heat-transfer-film/).
United States Fab Lab Network. "Fab Labs Are Global."
Retrieved March 21, 2016 (http://usfln.org/index.php/fab-
lab-ecosystem/fab-labs-are-global).

Index

About the Author

Cathleen Small is an author and editor living in the San Francisco Bay Area. She has written extensively for readers in grades K–12 and edited numerous nonfiction titles. When she's not reading or writing, Cathleen enjoys spending time with her two school-age sons, doing DIY home renovation, and traveling.

Photo Credits

Cover Ikonoklast Fotografie/Shutterstock.com; p. 5 The Boston Globe/Getty Images; p. 7 The Washington Post/Getty Images; p. 10 © Ann Hermes/Christian Science Monitor/The Image Works; p. 13 Mandel Ngan/AFP/Getty Images; p. 15 Predrag Vasilevski/Shutterstock.com; p. 20 Construction Photography/Alamy Stock Photo; p. 21 Moreno Soppelsa/Shutterstock.com; pp. 24-25 ChiPubLib Makerspace/Flickr/https://www.flickr.com/photos/cpl_makerspace/10040799845/CC BY-SA 2.0; p. 26 dinodentist/Shutterstock.com; pp. 28-29 © iStockphoto.com/LifesizeImages; p. 34 Learn 2 Teach, Teach 2 Learn, South End Technology Center @ Tent City; p. 36 Eric Hernandez/Getty Images; p. 39 Mara008/Shutterstock.com; p. 41 © iStockphoto.com/Thomas Demarczyk; p. 44 © B.O'Kane/Alamy Stock Photo; p. 47 Courtesy of Emergency Floor; p. 50 Eric Raptosh Photography/Blend Images/Getty Images; cover and interior pages background pattern Slanapotam/Shutterstock.com.

Designer: Nicole Russo; Editor: Bernadette Davis;
Photo Researcher: Nicole DiMella